THE WILDLIFE OF
AMERICA

CLB 1783
This 1991 edition published by Portland House,
distributed by Outlet Book Company, Inc, a Random House Company,
225 Park Avenue South, New York, New York 10003.
© 1987 Colour Library Books Ltd, Godalming, Surrey, England.
All rights reserved.
Printed and bound in Hong Kong.
ISBN 0 517 63117 2
8 7 6 5 4 3 2

THE WILDLIFE OF
AMERICA

Photography By
TOM HALL

Text By
DAVID BLACK

PORTLAND HOUSE

The first European settlers found in the United States a land rich in natural resources. The woods teemed with game and the rivers, lakes and coastal waters with fish of all kinds. They also found here a people, the indigenous Indians, who reaped this rich harvest without detriment to the ecology. But the land was to suffer a dramatic turn as the continent was gradually opened to successive waves of settlers. The changes that have been wrought in the intervening years have been considerable, and in many parts the landscape is unrecognizable from its primeval state, with industry, urban sprawl and intensive agriculture all having taken their toll. But stretching as it does from east to west between two oceans, and extending from the cold forests of the north to the arid deserts and subtropical swamps of the south, the natural framework of the country is so vast and varied that it remains a fascinating country for its wildlife.

As elsewhere, the animal life is linked to vegetation, which in turn is dependent on the soils, topography and climate. Although the belts of vegetation have been modified by man's activities, they are still apparent and extensive, and each one harbors its own distinctive wildlife.

The Eastern Forests

The hardwood forests of the northeast and of the Appalachian Mountains lie within easy distance of major conurbations. The climate and country is for the most part equitable enough to visit, camp in and backpack through, and to many Americans it represents the nearest thing to wilderness, even though one has to be lucky to find woods in their untouched, virgin state. Where they do exist they are tranquil and beautiful places where one can take a glimpse back into the past, to see how it used to be. This is a region of oak and hickory trees, of walnut, sweet gum and enormous, straight-limbed tulip trees.

The trees are swathed with enormous creepers of poison ivy and wild grape, and flowering dogwood opens its white or pink flowers in the late spring. From rocky bluffs sprout feathery ferns, and logs are carpeted with thick, spongy moss. It is under some of these logs that the area reveals its unusual animal riches, for the northeastern United States is the headquarters of the salamanders of the world, with up to 30 species.

The red-backed salamander is one of a dozen common woodland species. It lays its eggs in some damp recess, the female curling her body protectively around the eggs until they hatch. Other salamanders are rare, such as the red-cheeked salamander that lives only within the boundaries of the Great Smoky Mountain National Park in Tennessee.

In springtime, an invasion of warblers from the south feed on the rich insect pickings. These small birds are furtive as they scour the foliage, and are often difficult to see. More noticeable are the blue jays, aggressive, noisy birds with startling blue, white and black plumage. They raid other birds' nests and hide acorns for their winter store, but are surprisingly reticent when near their own nest, a bulky, ragged structure made of twigs. Up in the leafy canopy a brilliant flash of red signals a scarlet tanager, the male bird, for the female has much muted colors.

The forest is the home of white-tailed deer, especially where there are grassy clearings. Its summer coat is a rich reddish brown with white underparts; in winter it becomes a greyish brown. Deer feed on a wide range of plant food, from beech mast and acorns to twigs and buds. Signs of deer are more obvious than the animals themselves because they are nocturnal in habit, bedding down just before dawn. In winter, their trails form a network of interlocking tracks which, when concentrated, are known as "deer yards." Although their main predator, the cougar, has disappeared from these parts, when the deer die of starvation their bodies are eagerly feasted on by a host of smaller predatory animals such as coyote, fox, opossum, raccoon and mink.

At night, flying squirrels emerge from their daytime resting places, often abandoned woodpecker holes. By extending the fold of skin stretched between forelegs and hindlegs, the squirrel can sail through the air from the top of one tree down onto the trunk of a neighbouring one without touching the ground. The porcupine, another nightime feeder, rests by day in a hollow log. It feeds on the bark of trees as well as on green plants such as the fat skunk's cabbage. A beauty of the night is the pastel green luna moth, with its long-tailed hind wings. These large moths often flap against the mosquito netting of country houses during warm summer evenings. The moth's large green-and-yellow-striped caterpillar feeds on the leaves of forest trees such as chickory and sweet gum.

Pines, Marsh and Swamp

Bordering the hardwood forests to the south is a vast, flat region of pine forests which, near the coast, is interspersed with bogs and marshes. The New Jersey Pine Barrens are a wilderness of stunted oaks and pines, with an understory of huckleberry and bilberry, built on poor, acidic soil.

The region is interesting for its carnivorous pitcher plants and sundew, and for the beautiful Pine Barrens tree frog that is threatened with extinction as the area is drained.

Along the North Carolina coast lies extensive marshland, where red-winged blackbirds dance over the cane stems. In the thickest parts, the harvest mouse builds its spherical, woven nest and lives by balancing and gripping on to the stems with its long prehensile tail as it feeds on the flowers, seeds and shoots of the reeds and grasses. Another mammal, the muskrat looks like a large rat with webbed feet and, like its larger relative, the beaver, builds lodges that can be up to 10 feet across.

In Georgia the marvelous wilderness of the great Okefenokee Swamp has great cypress trees up to 150 feet high, with buttress "knees" that stick up out of the water. Here are dangerous water moccasins and enormous alligator snappers, both reptiles feeding on the fish that include cigar-shaped gars, and bowfin. Water birds abound, each having a different fishing tactic. For example, the Louisiana heron actually attracts fish to it by raising one wing to create a shadow, sticking its head underneath the wing to see if a fish has settled, then darting its head out and spearing the fish with its dagger-like beak. Side creeks have colonies of ibis, and fish hawks circle overhead.

The other famous wetland area is the Everglades of Southern Florida. Despite its reputation as a swampy wilderness, it is only waterlogged during the rainy summer season, when the whole area teems with life.

Picking their way on their wide-splayed toes over lily pads that crowd the water's surface are brilliant-coloured gallinules, whose plumage is a dazzling mixture of iridescent blues, purples and greens. Crakes, rails and herons utter their rasping calls as they squabble for territory and food.

In winter all the aquatic life drains off into the deeper channels. Here lurk alligators in a semi-torpid state, surrounded by their normal prey of gars and large-mouthed bass. The small mosquito fish is numerous, feeding on the aquatic larvae of these harmful insects which can be a real hazard to anyone venturing into the swamps unprotected.

Mangrove swamps fringe the Florida coast, their tangled proproots providing shelter for young fish that use them as nursery feeding grounds. This is the realm of the manatee, a large aquatic mammal with small foreflippers and an enormous, paddle-like tail. Munching its way through pounds of waterweeds each day, the manatee helps open up small waterways that have been clogged up with plants, especially the rampant water hyacinth. These aminals are becoming rare now, as they fall prey to boat propellers or are shot for food or sport, despite their being on the endangered list.

Grasslands

A few hundred years ago rolling grasslands stretched uninterrupted from the eastern forests all the way to the Rocky Mountains. No other region has suffered more from man's activities than the tallgrass prairies. Dominated by tall bluestem grass that reaches heights of 8 feet, these grasslands were once famous for their spectacular late summer displays of sunflowers, aster, goldenrod and cone flowers. Barely one percent of this lush area remains, frequented by the hardiest of prairie animals, the burrowing rodents. The pocket gopher lives a mainly underground life, digging enormous branching tunnel systems that can stretch 100 feet or more. It lives mainly on the roots of grasses which it strips off from below, using its oversized front incisor teeth. Franklin's ground squirrel is more of a surface feeder and supplements its plant diet with the young of ground-nesting birds. Both rodents fall prey to an animal that has the concentrated power of a mechanical exacavator: the badger, a squat, broad animal equipped with clawed forefeet and enormous, shovel-like hind ones. It scents out its prey and conserves its energy by sinking a series of vertical shafts, thus trapping the animals along the length of their runways.

A rare, evocative member of the tallgrass community is the greater prairie chicken. In springtime, the male inflates its orange throat sacs and produces a great booming sound to attract the females.

There is more remaining midgrass prairie to the west that runs like a narrow ribbon through the Dakotas, Nebraska, Kansas and Oklahoma. This is prairie dog country. The black-tailed prairie dog is a sociable animal, but the scale of its activities is hard to believe. One colony can contain several thousand animals and some of their "towns" are thought to have stretched over 200 hundred miles and may have contained hundreds of thousands of members. Their burrows have a characteristic conical entrance mound which prevents them from flooding and gives the animals that extra lift to look out for danger from all quarters – hawks in the air and badgers, bobcats and coyotes on the ground. Prairie dogs communicate with each other using a whole repertoire of chirps, chatters and squeals, and greet each other with "kissing" gestures, all these serving as recognition signals and helping maintain the cohesive nature of the colony.

In a region devoid of large trees, abandoned prairie dog burrows are regularly taken over by rattlesnakes, rabbits, field mice and the burrowing owl, a curious bird whose range extends southwards to the pampas of Argentina.

The shortgrass prairie to the west is an upland steppe with low rainfall, hot summers and winter temperatures well below freezing. Grasses and other plants have to be tough to survive here. A widespread plant is the fringed sagebrush, which provides an important food source for larger animals such as mule deer and pronghorn antelope. The resilient cactus pear also thrives, its succulent fruits eaten by jackrabbits as well as the largely carnivorous coyote.

This glimpse of the prairies gives the impression of a dry, even landscape, but the whole region is pockmarked with pools and marshes that act like magnets each spring to many thousands of waterfowl. At least fifteen species of duck regularly breed here, including pintail, canvasback, teal, scaup and redhead. During the breeding season these small patches of water are alive with the calls and activity of these birds, making them a bonanza for naturalists, especially birdwatchers.

Carved into the prairie plateaus are also creeks that wind through the grasslands, their banks lined with wide-spreading cottonwood trees and hackberry shrubs with their edible fruits. Bitterns and rails nest in the fringing reedbeds, and magpies flit between trees where they build their bulky, impregnable nests.

Mountains High and Wide

An imposing backdrop to the prairies are the Rocky Mountains that in places rise from hot, dry valleys up to snow covered peaks. They are not just one continuous range, but two distinct mountain blocks separated by the almost circular, scrub-covered Wyoming Basin. Climbing up through the mountains is equivalent to traveling many hundreds of miles to the north as scrub gives way to forest and, as the forest thins out at the timberline, alpine tundra takes over.

On the arid slopes of the southern mountains grows a dwarf forest of pinon pines and junipers. The nuts and fruits of these trees are avidly sought out by the pinon jay, a steel-blue bird that forages in noisy flocks. At night the ringtail raccoon comes out of hiding to hunt small rodents. The raccoon is an attractive animal with

a long, bushy rail broken up into 16 bands of black and white fur. It hunts by stealth, taking also insects, scorpions and juniper berries. When threatened, the ringtail screams and secretes a foul smelling fluid from a gland under its tail.

Chaparral covers other dry upland slopes, made up of dwarf oaks and drought-resistant, evergreen, prickly shrubs. Another jay makes its home here, the scrub jay that feeds on acorns. Mule deer also visit the chaparral zone in the fall to partake of the rich acorn crop. At this time the bobcat, a fierce predator, will often ambush young deer on their well-worn feeding tracks that snake through the otherwise impenetrable scrub.

Above the scrubby foothills real forest trees take over. Slopes of ponderosa pine form open parkland where squirrels nibble cones and mountain bluebirds flit between clearings, flashing across the glades to and from their nest holes. Eroded areas are quickly colonised by aspen seedlings that form beautiful, light leaved groves. Here beavers are industrious, building their great lodges and damming the mountain streams.

The wet, north-facing slopes support forests of Douglas fir with blue grouse, hawks and owls, while higher up, on the drier slopes, there are dense stands of lodgepole pine – this is black-bear country. An inquisitive, intelligent animal, the black bear roams large distances in search of berries, insects, fish and small mammals. In the tall, straight-trunked fir trees nest hairy woodpeckers, while crossbills feed on the cones, extracting the fir seeds with their uniquely equipped crossed mandibles.

Upward towards the treeline, mountain streams, cold water lakes and alpine meadows all create their own special wildlife areas. Rock slides are especially interesting as they are home to two special mountain mammals, the pika, a chunky looking, short-eared animal related to the rabbit, and the yellow-bellied marmot, a high altitude relative of the woodchuck. Whereas the marmot grows fat during the summer months in preparation for its winter sleep, the pika stores its winter food supply of grasses, specially set out to dry on the hot rock slopes. The marmots, in particular, are prey to golden eagles that nest high up on inaccessible crags.

One of the best places to view the mountain wildlife is in Yellowstone National Park in northwestern Wyoming. This is the oldest protected region in the United States, established in 1872, and is also the largest, covering over 3000 square miles of spectacular scenery, with bighorn sheep, elk, moose, bear and buffalo.

Desert Lands

Wedged between mountain blocks in the southwestern states are hot deserts of rock and sand. They are remarkable for their strange cacti and incredibly diverse animal life. In the spring, after a wet winter, the Mohave Desert is brilliant with wildflowers that shoot forth flower and set seed all in the space of a few weeks. This desert's most famous plant is the Joshua tree, a giant yucca that takes many decades to reach maturity, with its strange, limb-like branches. Naturalist's find these plants especially rewarding as many kinds of animals depend on them for food and shelter. Wood rats build their huge nests of desert debris at their bases. The rats feed on the young green leaves of the plant as well as on the succulent fruits of the cacti. Flickers and ladder-backed woodpeckers excavate nest holes in the branches, these in turn producing prime sites for a succession of birds from flycatchers and wrens to sparrow-hawks.

A food chain dependent on the Joshua tree starts with termites eating the wood. These insects are the main diet of the delicate yucca night lizard, which in turn itself falls prey to snakes and owls. A red-tailed hawk will often choose the Joshua's spreading limbs as a suitable nest platform, as will the black and yellow Scott's oriole that builds its nest right in amongst the spiky foliage.

In a similar way, giant saguaro and fuzzy coated cholla cacti dominate the Sonoran desert to the south. The saguaro's large, white, waxy flowers are pollinated by bats and white winged doves attracted by the rich nectar source.

The region is rich in reptiles, including the poisonous Gila monster, a fat lizard whose body is covered with pink and black bead-like scales. The chuckwalla, another large lizard, spends its days basking on sun-baked rocks.

Many animals, especially the small rodents, avoid the desert heat by being active at night, when other animals are afoot: hunters in the form of owls, spotted skink and snakes such as the sidewinder that moves in sidelong loops, leaving tell-tale J-shaped tracks in the sand.

The Pacific Coast

The Pacific coastal region can boast two gigantic plants. The first, giant seaweeds called kelp, grows off the coast of Central and Southern California, and attains lengths of up to 200 feet. Divers find kelp beds enchanting places; true underwater forests with over fifty common species of fish such as moray eels, giant seabass of up to 400 pounds, scorpionfish, and a sea perch known as rubberlips. The natural predators on these kelp forests are spiny purple sea urchins that rasp away at the tough brown fronds. They used to be kept in check naturally by sea otters that fed on them in large numbers, but as the sea otter nearly died out from over hunting, urchins have thrived. However, the sea otter has been reintroduced along the coast, and in places keeps the urchins in check. Unfortunately, the otter also likes to feed on abalones, shellfish popular in restaurants, and because of this it has come into conflict with the abalone harvesters.

It's worth mentioning that there is another large if not gigantic specimen in the region, the elephant seal. This marine mammal, up to 18 feet long, breeds on several islands off the coast of Baja California, where the male establishes a harem of smaller females.

The other true giants are the trees. In Northern California are groves of giant redwoods that grow along the coastal mountain chain, the forests maintained by the warm mists and fogs that daily roll over the hills from the ocean. Some trees can measure over 350 feet, and have been estimated to be over three thousand years old. The most famous animal inhabitants of these stands are the mountain beaver and the shrew-mole, whose closest relative lives in the Asian Far East.

North into Oregon and Washington there are many mighty specimens of spruce and fir. These lush forests have a cathedral-like stillness and wildlife is not easy to see, although they harbour herds of elk and the large, crow-sized pileated woodpecker, which hammers its way into tree trunks in its search for wood-boring insects.

This short account of the wildlife of the United States just touches on and gives a flavor of the natural wealth of the continent. Treasures today protected for all time in a superb network of national parks and monuments, where one can enjoy the wonderful scenery and explore the rugged terrain and become part of the natural landscape. The national parks cover all the major natural regions, from forest and mountain to prairie and desert, and include such special places as the dark green forests of Black Hill National Park, South Dakota, to the gleaming gypsum sands of White Sands National Monument in New Mexico, with its specially evolved, pale-coloured small animals.

Left: the white variant of the great blue heron, its reflection shimmering in the rippled water. Below: Eco Pond and (bottom), a great egret. Overleaf: a rare sea otter (bottom left) in characteristic sleeping posture, floating on its back and wrapped in a strand of kelp, (top left) a seal colony basking in the California sunshine, (top right) a seal and pup, and (bottom right) seabirds in Alaska.

Right: completely at home in its surroundings, an alligator takes its ease among the vegetation of the Everglades' Corkscrew Swamp Sanctuary. Below: an immature little blue heron and (bottom) an anhinga producing its harsh cry.

Eat or be eaten in the reptile world. Above left: a northern Pacific rattlesnake swallows a garter snake and (above right) a pair of raccoons investigate a bull snake they have captured and killed. Although this particular snake is non-poisonous, it does vibrate its tail segments in menacing, rattlesnake fashion. Top: a northern ribbon snake extending its jaws to accommodate a frog it has caught. Facing page: (top) a bull snake and its prey – a deer mouse. Bull snakes are considered useful as they help keep the rodent population down. Bottom: a western blue racer about to strike a leopard frog.

Above: a black bear cub sharpening its claws on the bark of a tree and (top) inquisitive red fox kittens, their eyes barely open. Facing page: (top) young coyotes at the playful stage, exploring the world near their den, and (bottom) belying its adult nature, a lynx kitten at its most vulnerable.

This page: examples of the wide range of coloring to be found in the black bear. Facing page: (top) a sow black bear with twin cubs. Black bear cubs (bottom) spend over a year with their mother, only leaving when it is time for her to mate again.

These pages: a selection of the varied animals that make their home in Florida's Everglades. Top left: a wary river otter, (above, above left and left) alligators exhibiting their fearsome fascination, and (top) a brown pelican. Facing page: (top) a common moorhen, (center left) a great blue heron watching for fish beside the broad, lance-shaped leaves of pickerelweed, (bottom left) a roseate spoonbill feeding in the saltwater shallows of the coastal Everglades, and (bottom right) a male anhinga, nearly three feet long from bill to tail tip. Overleaf: a group of bighorn rams.

The black oystercatcher (left) is a breeding bird of the rocky Pacific coast, while the chukar partridge (above left) is an Asian bird introduced into North America. Above: a ptarmigan in summer plumage and (top) a Californian quail. Facing page: (top) wild turkeys in the snow, and (bottom) a ringneck pheasant.

Facing page: a wapiti, or elk stag, with a third-year set of antlers. These are shed in February or March, and a new set grows in April. With the arrival of heavy snows, wapiti come down off the high ground to the sheltered valleys. Top: a female wapiti with twin calves. Though a single offspring is usual, twins are not uncommon. Above: two wapiti stags browsing on grasses at the edge of the forest, and (left) a wapiti hind.

Top: an anhinga preening, its back-feathers fluffed, wings outstretched and tail fanned to dry. Left: nesting wood storks and (above) a great egret. Facing page: double-crested cormorants in a slash pine. Overleaf: (left) coyotes, (top right) a timber wolf and (bottom right) a red fox.

The most notable feature of Dall's sheep (these pages) is the ram's magnificent pair of massive, curved horns which, when viewed in profile, formed a huge "C" shape called a "curl." Ewes have shorter, more slender horns that curve only slightly. They are found in many of the Rocky Mountain states.

The purple gallinule (below), though more colorful, is very similar to the the common moorhen in its habits and hen-like call. Left: an anhinga in the branches of a southern willow and (bottom) roseate spoonbills feeding, their distinctive, flattened bills ideally suited to sifting through water and mud for the small marine life on which they feed. Facing page: a yellow-crowned night-heron.

Bighorn sheep (above left) give birth to their young in late May or early June. The result of the white-tailed deer doe's first pregnancy is usually a single fawn (above right, top and facing page top), surely one of the most delightful of the young animals of the forests and able to stand on its own within a few hours of its birth. Facing page bottom: pronghorns in the snow.

Above: a mountain bluebird at its nest hole, (top) a killdeer on its nest, (top right) a yellow-bellied sapsucker, just returned to its young with its beak full of insects and (right) a long-billed curlew chick. Facing page: (top left) a caliope hummingbird, (top right) Bewick's wren, (bottom right) a tree swallow and (bottom left) a yellow-headed blackbird.

The mobile and sensitive lips of the black bear (above) are used to advantage when the animal feeds on small items such as berries or tender young plant shoots. Facing page: black bears climb in a manner that consists of a series of quick bounds, grasping with their forepaws and pushing with their hind legs.

e anhinga's distinctive plumage (right) can
ome so sodden and bedraggled during its
uent underwater forays in search of food that it
nable to fly, and has to clamber and claw its
to a safe perch. At such times it is necessary for
bird to engage in prolonged preening and
ing of feathers (facing page and bottom). Below:
mmature great blue heron.

Top: young chipmunks, their eyes not yet open, huddled together in their tree stump nest, (left) Richardson's ground squirrel, an alert and inquisitive animal of the rolling prairies and (above) an adult chipmunk. Facing page: young opposums (top) may travel on their mother's back until they are three months old. Bottom: the American badger shows its powerful digging claws.

The nutria, or coypu (above), originated in South America and was introduced into North America purely because of its fine fur. The beaver (top) is a large, industrious rodent that can weigh up to 60 pounds. Muskrats (facing page) live in wetland areas and build domed houses.

Despite their name, not all black bears are black –
indeed brown varieties (facing page and above) are
quite common. Top: a black bear in a swampy
hollow and (left) feeding on late autumn berries.
Above left: a grizzly bear, easily identifiable by its
muscular shoulder hump, pads through the snow.

Top: a Louisiana heron, snowy egret and roseate spoonbills feeding in Big Cypress Swamp in the Everglades. Above: a Lousiana heron and (right and facing page bottom) the white variant of the great blue heron, found only in salt water from southern Biscayne Bay around the coast to Everglades City. Facing page top: an anhinga spreads its sodden wings to dry in the sun.

The badger (top) eats a wide range of animals, including snakes. Pikas (above left) are small, tailless creatures, rather like guinea pigs in appearance, that live above the treeline in the Rocky Mountains, and the hairy marmot (above right) likes areas strewn with large boulders. Facing page: the white-footed mouse (top) is an uncommon creature, found only in dry, eastern deciduous forests, while the yellow-bellied marmot (bottom) is an animal of rocky hillsides.

Above: the long-billed curlew pictured backlit against a clear blue sky, its distinctive cinnamon underwing lining particularly evident. The great blue heron (remaining pictures) is one of the largest members of the heron family. Herons are most often found near water, usually lakes and rivers, but sometimes along the sea shore.

Columbian ground squirrels (top, above and facing page) excavate an elaborate tunnel system with a central chamber which is lined with soft plant seeds and grasses. Tunnels radiate from the central chamber to exit near the animals' feeding grounds. Like other ground squirrels, they carry seeds in their cheek pouches to be stored in the burrow for later consumption. Another animal that creates equally complex tunnels and chambers is the black-tailed prairie dog (right), one of the most gregarious of mammals.

Raccoons (these pages) hunt, forage and scavenge for a wide variety of foods, including fish, oysters, insects, small mammals, birds and their eggs, and many fruits and plants. With the onset of the dry season in November, their abundant food supplies are drastically reduced and, together with their prey and predators, they search the dried-up prairies even for water. By the time the first spring rains come, in about May, many have died of thirst and starvation.

Magnificent birds of prey: (top left) the powerful golden eagle, which makes its home in mountain country, (top right) the red-tailed hawk, a hunter that soars high above the landscape, and (right) the prairie falcon, a bird that is found in dry, open country, as is (facing page top) Swainson's hawk. Above: marsh hawk eggs and nestlings. Facing page bottom: the bald eagle, a fish-eating bird that also takes sick ducks and game birds.

Large bull elk (top) generally separate from the cow herds in the winter to spend the season apart. Above: young elk on the alert at the forest edge. Facing page: (top) a bull elk escorting his cows into the denser reaches of the forest (bottom).

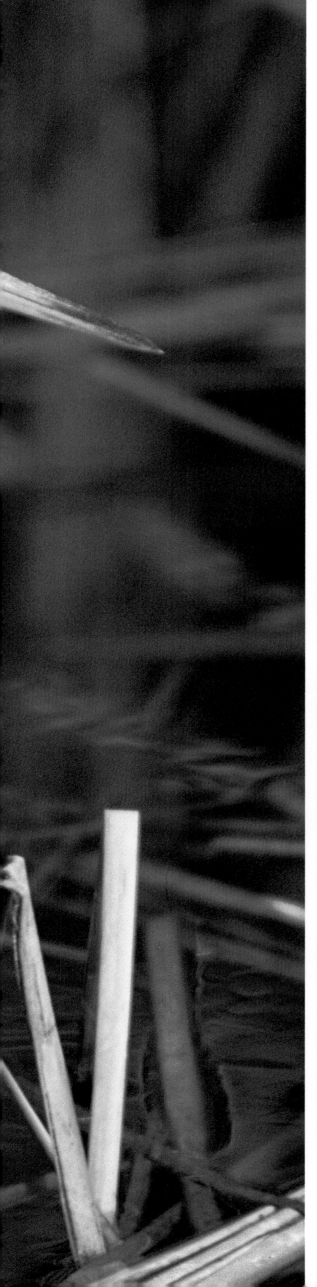

Offspring of the largest of the North American herons, an immature great blue heron (bottom) may grow to an adult height of four feet. The Louisiana heron (left) feeds along saltwater shores, in company with the white ibis (below). White ibis often congregate in large flocks, flying in long lines or in V-formation. Different types of heron and other water birds will readily share both feeding and nesting grounds, and noisy, untidy, mixed rookeries are a distinctive feature of cypress and mangrove forests.

Black bears (these pages) usually stand a little less than three feet high at the shoulder. They will often climb trees to rest, to feed, or to escape danger, and will rub themselves against tree trunks to relieve itching.

Gator holes, such as that (below) at Big Cypress Swamp, provide vital catchments for the fast-disappearing water during the winter dry season and sustain a wide variety of wildlife until the spring rains. Left: pond apple trees and (bottom pictures) a water moccasin.

lligators (these pages) mate in April and May, during
hich time the bulls will fight (facing page bottom). The
male builds a nest of weeds and rotting leaves, raised
to a mound above the water, where she lays up to
xty eggs in late May or early June. Incubated by the
at of the sun and the decomposing vegetation, the
gs hatch after about sixty-five days to release
iniature alligators approximately nine inches long.
elow: a young alligator.

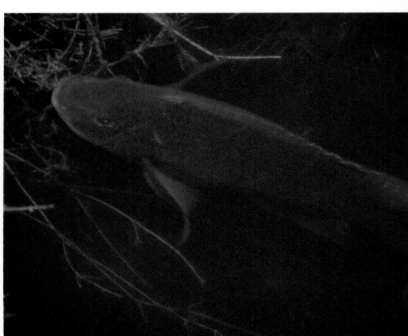

Top: the broad, blunt snout of an alligator, one of the many which inhabit the Everglades' complex system of lakes, sloughs and swamps. The common moorhen (left and facing page) is found in freshwater ponds and marshes and feeds at the edge of open water, ready, if disturbed, to seek shelter in bordering vegetation.

Vocalization takes many different forms in the animal world. The black bear (top) can growl, squeal and grunt, while the cougar (facing page bottom), like all cats, growls, hisses and purrs, and the bull elk (facing page top) bellows out a high-pitched roar, or bugle. Above: a bobcat snarls threateningly, exposing its sharp teeth. The howl of the wolf (right) is one of the signs of the true wilderness.

The golden eagle (facing page) is distinguished by its strong, hooked beak, overall brown plumage and feathered legs. Favorite hunting grounds are foothills with grassy pastures, where prey such as the yellow-bellied marmot may be found. Remaining pictures: an eagle with its marmot prey.

The raccoon (bottom right), seen here hunting warily in Corkscrew Swamp Sanctuary, flourishes in almost every habitat to be found in the Everglades. Right and bottom: alligators emerge from the water to sun themselves, thus raising their externally-controlled body temperature. Below and bottom: dense surface-coverings of water lettuce, a major source of the dead vegetation continually being laid down in the Everglades as a rich, organic peat.

The coyote (left) has a narrow chest, long legs and a slender muzzle. Top: a wolf walks stealthily through hard-packed snow, its loosely-held tail an indication of relaxation. Like dogs, wolves are unable to perspire in the usual way, and pant (above) in warm weather. Facing page: (top) a wolf beside its kill in a clearing and (bottom) a watchful wolf and its prey, a young Hereford calf.

Stellar's sea lion, or the northern sea lion (facing page), occurs in its largest numbers in the Gulf of Alaska. They spend most of their lives at sea, coming ashore in May to form breeding colonies, in which they stay for about three months. A male Stellar sea lion (left) may weigh up to 2,200 pounds. Above and top: gulls, the most common birds of the coast.

Slider turtles (bottom right) dig themselves into the moist undersoil at the onset of the dry season, and there survive the drought in a state of aestivation – a condition akin to hibernation, but not as deep or sustained. During particularly severe drought even the reservoir-like 'gator holes may prove insufficient, and alligators (remaining pictures and overleaf) will aestivate in damp dens adjoining their dried-up waterholes.

Measuring up to eight feet from nose to tail, the magnificent polar bear (these pages and overleaf) is justifiably regarded as the "King of the North." Beautiful though they may appear, however, polar bears are also immensely powerful creatures of the wilderness, and have on many occasions demonstrated just how dangerous they can be, particularly in the case of a female guarding her cubs (overleaf bottom left).

Alaska, America's largest state, is home to a wide variety of wildlife (these pages), including the grizzly bear (pictures above and above right), caribou (top right and facing page top and bottom), moose, the largest member of the deer family (right) and the familiar horse (facing page center).

In summer caribou (left) feed on a range of plants, but in winter they exist mainly on lichens. Moose (remaining pictures) are solitary animals for the most part, coming together in groups only during the winter. They feed on a wide range of vegetation, including water plants.

Facing page: a saw-whet owl, its prey firmly clutched in its talons, and (above) an adult male snowy owl, its over-all coloring making it easily distinguishable from the immature (above right). Right: the round, yellow eyes of the great horned owl, looking as full of wisdom as folklore suggests, and (top) the bird with its prey, a snowshoe hare.

Facing page: (top) a cow moose and calf. Needing up to sixty pounds of food each day means that some moose are unable to survive particularly severe winters. Bottom: the pronghorn's coarse winter coat affords it a considerable degree of protection against biting winds. Above: the caribou's survival during the harsh winters may well depend on its ability to detect food lying under several inches of snow. Overleaf: far from the north of the country, a raccoon in the Florida Everglades.

Above: cougar cubs. Young cougars stay with their mothers for up to two years. Top and facing page: a pair of older cubs, showing the animals' beautiful fur coloring. Right: a yawning cougar displaying the large, pointed teeth typical of a carnivore.

Right and facing page: rattlesnakes about to strike, their bodies coiled and tensed and their rattles clearly vibrating. Top: a bullsnake and rattler in a tug-of-war battle over a mouse. Rattlesnakes generally make their homes in dry, desert-like areas, and should they be caught in the open (above), are quite unable to survive extreme cold. Overleaf: a small herd of elk, led by the dominant male, heads for the shelter of the forest.

The black widow spider (left), although able to inject venom that would certainly cause considerable distress to humans, is not quite the deadly creature of folklore. The fluffy, ball-like egg case can contain as many as 750 eggs, from which the young spiders emerge in 14-30 days.

The swallowtail butterfly, so-named because of the hindwings' tail-like extensions, is found in many places throughout the world. There are many color and pattern varieties, the tiger swallowtail (above) being a particularly aptly-named specimen. Facing page: the garden spider (top) is a member of the family of orb weavers, so-named for their characteristic web (bottom).

Despite its ferociously-hooked beak, the bald eagle (these pages) is more of a scavenger than an active hunter. Its primary food consists of dead fish washed up on the shores of the sea, lakes or rivers. It has declined in numbers and is now more common on the Pacific coast. The nests, built in tall trees, may become huge as the birds often return and add to them year after year.

Top: an unusual, and surely less than serious, "combat" between a moose and a mule deer. Above: a bull moose picking its way through fresh snow and (facing page top), foraging for subsistence in the deep snow. Facing page bottom: a bull moose displaying the stump of its new antlers.

The western spotted frog (right) spends most of the summer in and around water, and the painted turtle (top) is common in weedy ponds and lakes and can often be seen sunning itself on a log. Above: a tussock moth caterpillar crawls up a log invaded by slime mold fungus and (facing page) a bumblebee searches for nectar on the flowerhead of a member of the thistle family.

Facing page: (top) a badger and (bottom) a red fox vixen display formidable sets of teeth. Play is important for young red foxes (top) as it teaches them to develop their hunting skills. Above: its face covered in dirt, a badger emerges after underground tunneling. Left: a bighorn ram in dominant pose.

The osprey (left and facing page bottom) is a bird of prey that builds its nest in tall trees near water. It lives almost exclusively on fish, which it snatches from or near the surface in its sharp talons. The American avocet (top and facing page top) calls an alarm-like "kleep" when disturbed. Its preferred habitat is near shallow lakes and sloughs. The herring gull (above) is a universal scavenger.

When stalking prey, cougars (above and top) move with extraordinary stealth. Facing page: the cougar's soft markings blend in well with various habitats.

acing page top: a wary river otter and (facing page ottom) a water moccasin. Above: a roseate spoonbill fting the water with its broad, flattened bill, (top) a tle blue heron watching the weed-covered surface and ight) a great blue heron among overhanging willow.

Above: an elk calf with its typical, spotted coat, born in late May or early June. Facing page: mountain caribou (top) give birth to their fawns in mid June, in hilly terrain. Bottom: plains buffalo calves are a bright reddish tan when newly born.

Top: a black bear eyes proceedings warily, while (facing page) a grizzled specimen does the same from a bed of horsetail plants. Above: a sow black bear and her yearling cub investigate a deer carcass.

Once widely distributed throughout the North American arctic region, the musk ox (above) is now limited to Alaska and some Arctic Ocean islands. The wood bison (top) may stand as high as seven feet at the shoulder. Facing page: a plains bison in a blizzard. The massive head acts as an efficient snow plough, enabling the animal to get at the vegetation underneath.

Elk portraits. Top: combat between elk stags includes shoving with their antlers, which seldom lock as do those of moose, caribou and deer. They may also lash at each other with their forefeet, rising up on their hind legs to do so. Facing page bottom: a victorious bull.

Top: a cougar stretches to scratch its head on a thorn bush, showing the full extent of its long, lithe, powerful body. Males may reach nine feet, including the long, cylindrical tail. When cougar cubs (facing page top) are about six weeks old the mother introduces them to a meat diet. Overleaf: (top left) a coyote, (bottom left) an Arctic fox, (top right) northern timberline wolves and (bottom right) a red fox.

The bobcat (facing page) is not hunted to any extent for its fur, which is soft and not very durable. The lynx (top and above) molts its long guard hairs in the spring and in the fall. Overleaf: in a snowstorm, elk stags engage antlers in a battle of strength for dominance over a harem of females.

Previous pages: the Pacific rattlesnake (top left) at a den entrance, (bottom left) mating and (top right) swallowing a mouse. Bottom right: a snake's tongue acts as an extremely effective sense organ. Rocky Mountain rams (these pages) spend a lot of time fighting with each other for dominance within the all-male herd or, during the winter rutting period, clashing horns to win the females.

Clark's nutcracker (top and facing page) feeds on nuts and conifer seeds. Above: a male mountain bluebird at its nest in an abandoned woodpecker hole, (above right) the gray jay of the northern forests, and (right) Stellar's jay.

Top and facing page: in the fall a victorious and dominant stag elk advertises himself by a bellowing call known as bugling. Above: an elk stag with growing antlers covered in velvet.

Although it hunts mainly by night, the cougar (these pages) is active throughout the day. It is an all-purpose hunter that can live in a variety of habitats and is quick to defend its young – and its food – from intruders.

A distinctive feature of the golden eagle (facing page and above left) is the yellow, fleshy cere at the base of the bill, which is nearly as long as the bird's head. Top: a red-tailed hawk mantling its prey, (left) a fledgling red-tailed hawk and (above) a goshawk, a bird of forest edges and clearings.

Left: a whitetail deer buck. Making its home, for preference, at the edges of hardwood forests, this is probably the most widespread game animal of North America. Top: a mule deer buck and (above) a doe mule deer, in deep snow. Facing page: (top) mule deer bucks in rut, and (bottom) young mule deer bucks, their breath making clouds of vapor in the cold air.

Canada geese (these pages) prefer to nest, in America, in the northwestern states. A pair with the young of that year are inseparable. The female leads the way, followed by the young, with the gander bringing up the rear. The young fly south with their parents in the fall and do not separate from them until they return the following spring to the nesting grounds.

Facing page: a mule deer buck. During the summer the bucks live in high alpine meadows. Antlers are carried only by the male and are shed in the spring. Top: a mule deer doe and fawn and (left) a doe mule deer with a grizzled, brown winter coat. In winter, mule deer travel in mixed herds led by an experienced doe. The rut of the whitetail deer (above) starts in mid October and continues until late December. Overleaf: a whitetail deer on the alert for the safety of her fawn.